Cut Wedding Costs -
Before The Big Day

Book 1:
Over 80 Ways To Save Money, Time and Frustration...
Before Your Big Day

By
Keith Maderer

Part of the:

K.Ì.S.S.S.
Keeping It Simple - Single Solutions
S E R Ì E S

Website:
KeithMaderer.com
Amazon Author Page

ISBN-13: 978-1542815673
ISBN-10: 1542815673

Special Free Offer

Get your

Free Video Training:
Wedding Day - Time Savers & Checklist

excerpt from this book - by clicking here:

http://kdmaderer.evsuite.com/cutweddingcosts1/

Introduction:

The Problem...

Getting married can be as simple as getting your license, taking a blood test, getting two witnesses and heading off to the justice of the peace.

Total cost... a few hundred dollars.

But in reality, most young couples would prefer to have a nice ceremony and a fun reception party with family, friends and co-workers that are close to them. The cost for such an endeavor has continued to rise over the years and the average 200 guest wedding in an average city can cost between $25,000 to $35,000 based on current estimates.

That amounts to $125 to $175 per person that attends your wedding. These figures include everything from the wedding gown, tuxedos, church and officiant costs, hall rental, food, alcohol, dessert, photographer, music and dozens of smaller items that will arise.

Let us not forget the additional cost of engagement and wedding rings which are added to the above costs.

So How Do We Pay For All of That?

Here is the problem that faces most young couples. How do we come up with the $25,000 or more to afford a nice wedding. The wedding of our dreams... mostly the bride's point of view. From a groom's standpoint, less is better. Especially if that bill is being paid for entirely by the couple.

The Solution...

The good news is that if you communicate early, plan properly, and are willing to be flexible, you can have a wonderful, memorable and special wedding. Even better, not put yourself in debt to pull it off.

In this book you will find out the most effective ways to open the wedding communication pipeline, establish a reasonable budget, execute your plan and find plenty of ways to be flexible in each category of wedding expenses.

You will find ways to make your day great and have the most fun possible within the budget that you establish. These wedding cost savers will show you a variety of ways to treat yourself and your guests to a great experience and a memorable day... for less.

What Do I Know ???

Why should you listen to me? I have been very fortunate to work with hundreds of clients over the years. As a financial adviser, I talk about money openly with clients every day. Each and every one of them has taught me something, in some area.

I also have five adult children that are getting engaged, married and starting their own families. I have also been blessed with many friends that are part of that young adult, young family or just getting started... age group.

I am a sponge when it comes to learning ways to help others... and myself, save money. For years I have taken notes as people share their best wedding cost savings secrets and strategies.

I have gone on to share those with many others as well. In this book, I will share those same secrets, strategies, research and wisdom with you.

Could you find this information elsewhere on your own? Sure... some of it. But it would take hundreds of hours of research over many weeks or months and I guarantee you would still miss many of the items that I have compiled for you.

You get it all in this short book. For just a few dollars.

My Promise to You...

If you are not completely satisfied with the tips, strategies and savings that you achieve by utilizing the solutions and ideas in this book, just send me an email at keith@keithmaderer.com and request a full refund.

All you need to do is send a copy of your paid receipt for the book along with your name, address and phone number. I will send you a full refund.

Yes... I am that confident that you will find value, savings and some great ways to enhance your wedding plans.

Take Action Now...

Don't wait until your plans are finalized and those bills come due. Get this book now. Find ways to cut costs without sacrificing your dreams. Explore your opportunities before decisions need to be made. Consider all your options and then pick and choose the items that suit your needs and your budget.

The money you save in one area could pay for one or more others that you never thought you could afford. Spend a few dollars now to get this compiled wisdom, advice and research in one place.

It will save you money. It will help you find ways to pay for the wedding of your choice. It will help you to take control of your wedding plans and customize them to meet your personal desires. You will make better decisions and have peace of mind knowing that your new life together was started on a strong foundation.

Your Challenge...

Each chapter of this book will offer multiple options, suggestions and strategies that you can use to focus your efforts and your finances into getting the most value for your dollars.

Take each category and review all the potential solutions, then sit down with your loved ones and discuss the alternatives. By keeping everyone that matters in the decision process, you will make stronger, better and easier choices.

Don't let others dictate how your wedding day will become a memory. Pick and choose the options that make you happy, that make your day special, and make your budget acceptable.

I believe in you and your ability to make it happen. Use these resources and make your wedding everything you want it to be.

Table of Contents

Why I Wrote This Book

So many young couples are being forced into debt to pay for their weddings.

In the past, the bride's parents paid for the wedding and the groom's parents paid for the rehearsal dinner.

Today, with costs for an average wedding in the range of $30,000... many families cannot afford to help their children. They may have helped with college, a car or maybe a house already... they just don't have the money available to pay for a wedding.

So how do these couples pay for their wedding?

They put it on credit and hope that the wedding gifts they receive (preferably checks and cash) will pay off their debts after the wedding.

Reality strikes when they add up their gifts and find out that there is not enough money to pay the bills or their credit cards.

They start their new life together with another debt and now have to add that bill to their already strained monthly budget.

This is the scenario that many newlyweds are facing today. For that one big party with all your family and friends... the **financial hangover** can last for years.

I wrote this book to help you make better decisions, openly discuss your alternatives and evaluate your resources.

I wrote this book to provide a variety of cost saving options that you can utilize if they make sense for your big day.

I wrote this book because I have helped many young couples learn the strategies that can make life enjoyable and remain affordable.

I wrote this book so you can get your new life started on a positive note and start building a wonderful future together.

You have in your hands a compilation of solutions, strategies and cost savers to help make great decisions and get the best value for your efforts.

Start planning your wedding by reading these strategies, evaluating your alternatives and cutting your wedding costs.

Let the fun begin....

Wedding Myths That Matter...

In Book One, we will share the seven myths that you need to know before you start planning your wedding. These will help you ask the right questions and interpret the answers you receive. In Book Two I will share six additional myths that you should review on your journey to, *Your Big Day*.

Myth 1: Bride's parents will pay for the whole wedding

With wedding costs rising each year, many couples are finding out that the bride's parents cannot afford to pay for the entire wedding. In many cases, they cannot, or will not be contributing anything to help out. Every families financial situation is different. While some families have planned to help with the wedding expenses, many have not.

Your best course of action is to sit down with your parents very early on in the wedding planning process. Ask if they were planning to help out in any way. If not, ask if they would be willing or able to help out financially.

So many young couples are afraid to ask and then the parents just assume it is all taken care of. The worst thing that can happen is they can say no. Either way, you will then know what you are dealing with and can begin planning and budgeting appropriately.

In most wedding scenarios, it is likely that if parents can help out, it will not be for the entire amount of the wedding. If you are lucky, you may be able to get a commitment where the brides' parents can pay one-third, the groom's parents can pay one-third and the wedding couple can manage the remaining one-third of the desired budget.

If parent's have arranged to provide a specific dollar figure (eg. $5,000, $10,000, etc) as their financial contribution, this can then be used to help build your budget in reverse.

The most important thing to remember is to ask. Communication and agreement are the key.

Myth 2: Groom's parents will pay for rehearsal party and dinner

Now that we have discussed Myth 1 above, Myth 2 falls right in line. If you have discussed the wedding finances with both sets of parents and come to an agreement, then who pays for the rehearsal party/dinner becomes a moot point.

Just make sure that when you are establishing your wedding budget, you build the rehearsal party costs into that budget.

The more open discussion that you have with your family about the wedding plans and budgets, the better off you will be as you get closer to the big day.

Myth 3: The size of your wedding party doesn't affect your budget

The number of bridesmaids and groomsmen can, and will affect your budget. Make sure that you set your budget before you begin officially asking family and friends to participate in your wedding party. A smaller wedding party will save dollars on flowers, gifts, hair, makeup, bachelor and bachelorette weekends or trips.

If you are not adding these items into your budget, you could be significantly over-spending by the time you reach your wedding day. With many younger guests, the more they have to spend to be in your wedding, this will reduce the amount that they give as a gift.

The larger your wedding party, means more expense, and potentially smaller gifts. That will impact your budget negatively on both sides. That is the reality, so beware.

It is also not mandatory that you have equal numbers of bridesmaids and groomsmen. Make sure that you ask those individuals that are important to you first and then stop the list there.

Myth 4: You were invited to <u>their</u> wedding... So you have to invite them to yours

Many young couples have the belief that if you are invited to someone's wedding, you are obligated to invite them to your wedding. This is not true.

When you are making up your list, only invite the people that you want to have at your wedding. Everyone perceives their relationships with others differently.

This can be as true for family members as it is for friends and co-workers. When it comes to family members, there always has to be a line as to how far out on the family tree you go. But sometimes it could be a close family member that never responds or attends anything. If you don't believe they should be invited, ask your parents. If all agree, leave them off.

Remember that your wedding day should be reserved for people that you an your immediate family feel are someone that would enjoy, celebrate, and encourage your marriage vows.

There will always be a few that you invite out of obligation, but try to minimize these guests as they usually do not participate in your festivities and end up complaining about something.

Myth 5: Your fiance will not care or have an opinion about the arrangements

Many brides-to-be believe that their fiance will agree with everything that they propose and just say... Yes dear. While this may happen in a few situations, the most likely scenario is the that there will be several specific items that your fiance will have a strong opinion on.

In order to avoid the tension and stress that will follow, make sure to include both parties in all of the decisions that relate to your wedding. It is a great idea to sit down once each week with a summary of ideas and planning that you have laid out and get initial agreement that you are both on the same page.

If there is a disagreement about something specific, each of you should offer 2-3 alternatives and then discuss which would best suit your situation. Remember that this is a marriage and a collaboration of ideas. There will be enough decisions to go around. Having an open mind and the ability to compromise will lead to a much better outcome and allow both parties to leave their mark on your new life together.

Myth 6: Everyone involved in planning your wedding will be happy and supportive

Wedding bliss and rose colored glasses can make everything look wonderful. All too often, wedding plans can be undermined by someone that is jealous, angry or envious of your new found happiness.

In many cases it is the people closest to you, your siblings, parents and wedding party that become an issue. Weddings have a funny way of triggering emotions that normally would not be exposed.

The best thing you can do is expect that some issues will arise and try to be open to the comments and empathetic to their situation. Try to add their input and accommodate their ideas while not letting it get in the way of your special day.

If you let them know that you care and are open to their suggestions or feelings, their attitude may change from problematic to supportive and then everyone will have a much more enjoyable time.

Myth 7: We don't need a wedding budget

Some young couples believe that a budget is unnecessary because they are planning to spend as little as possible on each area of importance. But what does that mean... as little as possible. It can vary from couple to couple, and even from bride to groom.

It will generally save you money if you review the online wedding calculators and all the different items that they list. Then sit down with your wedding focus group and prioritize your "wedding want", and "wedding need" list.

Wedding Focus Group: Your WFG should include the bride and groom, parents and siblings and any other close friends or individuals that you trust and would like involved. Their input is just there to help with the ideas and planning. Ultimately it is up to you to decide on your priorities.

A note about Online Wedding Calculators. While these are great tools to give you an overview of the process, they will not necessarily keep you on track. You have to take your priorities and build a budget that is realistic and affordable for your situation. No online calculator can do that for you.

Conclusion:

These are just some of the many wedding myths that young couples have been allowing to get in the way of an affordable and enjoyable wedding. Don't be unrealistic in your expectations. The more open-minded you are, the better your wedding plans, wedding day and married life will be.

In Book Two of this series - **Your Big Day and Beyond** - you will find the answers to the following myths and 8 additional chapters of Cost Savings Strategies:

Myth 8: You will pay a fortune on alcohol and drinks

Myth 9: Everything will be Perfect on your Wedding Day

Myth 10: My Priest or Clergy can perform the ceremony outside the Church

Myth 11: It is our day, our rules, our way... or the highway

Myth 12: No second thoughts

Myth 13: Drop 20 pounds before the wedding

Chapter 1: Ring Savers

The engagement and wedding rings can cost between $3,000 and $6,000 today. Even more if you are not careful. Somethings are more important the the ring size or dollar amount spent.

The majority of women said they would be happy with whatever engagement ring was chosen. They would rather you propose sooner than wait until you can afford a more expensive engagement ring.

While most bride's to be would rather have their fiance propose engagement with a smaller, less expensive ring than wait until you can afford that big rock. Many young men worry about the appearance of not impressing their bride-to-be, or her family, or friends.

Making an affordable purchase that is within your budget can help establish a great precedent for your love and start your marriage on a positive note.

If the woman of your dreams is only concerned with the size of the diamond on her hand, then maybe she isn't the true... woman of your dreams.

Most young couples are just establishing their careers and digging themselves out of student loan debt. The financial aspect of ring purchases needs to be a concern of both parties and should be openly discussed before deciding on the final engagement and wedding rings.

Forget the Archaic 3 Month Salary Rule:

This is a guideline that was established decades ago by jewelers in an effort to get you to pay more than necessary for your rings. Everyone has a different monthly salary, so why should you try to base your ring purchases on a number that could change from year to year or person to person. Is that salary before taxes or net? As you can see this rule is no longer relevant.

Everyone should set their own budget and try to find suitable rings at or below this figure. Surprisingly, I believe that you should look a the next section first, then set up your engagement and wedding ring budget based on your findings.

Buy online:

The overhead and high costs associated with having a retail brick and mortar store can add significantly to the cost of jewelry and especially to diamond engagement rings and other wedding sets. As Amazon.com has shown, online merchants can offer more price competition and still offer great quality and value.

Finding reputable online jewelers should be your first task. Ensuring that the purchase you make is documented, delivered and insured properly can be a challenge. The good news for you is that the list of online jewelry stores below is a great place to begin your ring shopping.

Try clicking the links below and take a look at their sites, inventory, educational resources, policies and prices. I think you will be _pleasantly surprised_ by what you find.

1. www.BlueNile.com – One of the first online diamond dealers, large selection

2. www.SuperJeweler.com – Some of the best prices and sales online

3. www.Ritani.com – High resolution images and free shipping

4. www.JamesAllen.com – High resolution images and free shipping

5. www.WhiteFlash.com – Large inventory of certified ideal and super ideal diamonds

6. www.b2cJewels.com – Low price guarantee and great customer service

7. www.Amazon.com – Search for women's bridal sets or engagement rings

8. www.GemVara.com – Great site for non-traditional engagement rings.

No matter which style, setting or cut you are looking for, you should be able to find something spectacular at a great price on one of these sites.

Don't Wait For Perfection:

Another way to achieve substantial savings on ring purchases is to accept minor flaws in weight, color and clarity. A lower grade of color or clarity can save a great deal of money and in most cases will not be differentiated by anyone without a jeweler's eye loupe magnifier.

While requesting a slightly smaller diamond or a slight difference in clarity and color, never sacrifice on the diamond's cut. Your cut is what will make the diamond sparkle and reflect light.

Consider Family Heirlooms:

Many individuals have been offered the gift of family heirloom jewelry that was handed down from parents, grandparents or even great grandparents. In many cases, this jewelry can be re-purposed, resized or even re-styled to make a beautiful engagement ring that would have extra special significance and tradition.

If you are fortunate enough to have access to these arrangements, please don't overlook the possibilities and savings that could be waiting for you. Explore the options and see what can be done. Don't forget to ask parents, grandparents etc. about this option. It may surprise you.

Consider Non-Traditional Settings and Shapes:

The perfect round diamond requires the highest cutting skills and cost of any diamond. By selecting one of the many other cuts, princess, oval, marquis, emerald or pear shape diamonds, your ring will stand out, be different and unique. It may also cost 25% to 50% less than the perfect round cut diamond.

By selecting a Halo Setting with a smaller center stone you can also have the appearance of a much larger diamond with a substantially lower overall cost. Explore the options that are provided on the various online resources and evaluate your needs based on what is available and what would make you happy. Being a little non-traditional can save a lot of money.

Consider a Different Stone:

Another great way to save on engagement and wedding rings is to select different gemstones instead of a diamond. In recent years, Sapphires, Rubies and even synthetic diamonds have become a much more popular choice. The great news about that is that you can have a beautiful, colorful ring with smaller diamonds surrounding the gemstone and it will save hundreds or even thousands of dollars.

Avoid Name Brand Rings:

Avoid buying rings that come with a pedigree. Zales, Veraggio, Tiffany, Bulgari, Cartier or any of the dozen's of other designer rings will cost more. You are paying for the name. Most any jeweler can create a custom design that will match or exceed your expectations. Do not get caught up in the designer name. Look a the quality and value for the money you are spending. The multitude of choices available from the online resources above are tremendous. I would be shocked if you cannot find something spectacular that your loved one and your budget, will both love.

Odd Carat Weights:

One of the most cost conscious ways to buy diamonds is to purchase carat weights that are just shy of the critical weights. As an example. If you are looking for a 1 carat diamond, try to find one that is .90 or .95 of a carat. This slightly smaller diamond will not be recognizable to most individuals and it could reduce your cost by as much as 20% to 35%.

The most common critical weights that are in demand are in ¼ carat increments. By selecting something that is just below those break points, you may save a bundle. Jewelers tend to discount these, "almost official weight" diamonds significantly when they receive them. In many cases they will receive more of these off-weight gems because it requires a larger stone and more detailed cutting to achieve perfect carat weight diamonds.

Don't allow the sacrifice of a smidgen of size to deter your purchase. Your loved one will appreciate the value and your budget will love the savings.

Don't let others tell you what to spend:

When it comes time to make your purchases, it seems that everyone has a rule, a guideline or they "know a guy" who will work with you. While you are more than welcome to listen to all these friends, pundits and experts... you should set your own budget based on your own financial situation.

No one knows your financial means better than you do. If you have taken the time to look at the overall cost of your desired wedding, researched your ring purchases properly and know what you are willing to spend, don't allow others to sway your thinking.

Stick to your Desired Budget:

By selecting engagement and wedding rings that fit within your desired budget, you will be able to monitor your spending and allocate funds to each area of your wedding and honeymoon expenses.

If you happen to exceed your budget in one area, or better yet, come in under-budget, then you are able to re-allocate funds in other areas that may surprise you later on in the planning.

Always remember... it is <u>your</u> hard earned money that you are spending for the goods and services required for your big day. If you are uncomfortable with the amounts, stop, reassess and look for alternatives until you are satisfied with your purchase.

Just Ask:

Once you have done your research and taken a look at the variety of rings that are available, reach out to a few of the local and online jewelry stores and ask them a question.

What is your best value ring for a slightly undersized diamond with a minor defect or clarity issue? (Or whatever other parameters that you are willing to accept.)

If they offer some suggestions, ask to get hi-resolution photos from online retailers and visit in person for local merchants. If you visually cannot detect the minor imperfections, most others will not either.

They may offer a few very appealing choices that will be acceptable and substantially discounted. Just make sure to get the proper paperwork and certifications on size, quality, etc. with your purchase.

Action Summary:

If you plan to save money on your engagement and wedding rings, you need to follow the guidelines above and be sensible about your purchases. First go to your local bridal shows and jewelry stores.

Look at a variety of rings and select the styles and shapes that fit your taste. Take photos of the top 3 choices at each of your 2 or 3 locations.

Get your ring sizes measured and take note of all the details, cut, color, clarity, carat weights and costs.

Then go to the online resources provided in this chapter and compare. Look for sales, clearance items and specials that would accommodate your desires and make an educated decision on what to purchase within your budget or less if possible.

Your $500.00 to $1,000.00 Challenge:

How can I (we) use this information to save at least $500.00 to $1,000.00 on our ring purchases?

Chapter 2: Dress/Gown Savers

Looking your best can be such a great, uplifting event for your big day. But if you have ever seen shows like "Say YES to the Dress", you know that dress prices can be outrageous. Set your budget and stay within it. For most women, the wedding dress will be worn once and then cleaned, stored and possibly forgotten... or even worse... lost or ruined.

That is what your wedding photos and video are for. Most young couples will see their wedding attire more in photos and video than they will in person. So be sure to place the proper perspective on your wedding attire. It can be a budget breaker... but it doesn't have to be. Here are some solutions that work great.

Rent It:

If you think purchasing a wedding dress that you will only wear once is a giant waste of money, then renting a beautiful dress may be just the answer for you... and your budget. There are plenty of resources available today and the list below represents some of the major players. If you Google – wedding dress rentals in "your hometown or city" - you will probably find some additional and surprising alternatives.

- www.renttherunway.com – Rent the Runway
- www.vowtobechic.com – Vow To Be Chic
- www.weddingtonway.com – Weddington Way rentals
- www.getthegown.com – Get The Gown
- www.llrental.com – L & L Rentals
- www.borrowingmagnolia.com – Borrowing Magnolia

Go Casual:

This is one of the easiest ways to achieve substantial savings. Look for a beautiful dress that really makes you look and feel great. Then find out if it comes in white, cream or whatever color you fancy.

These dresses can be short, long or even prom gowns. Many prom gowns come in white or cream, but usually are not stocked as prom dresses. You may have to order the color of your choice, but the cost can be substantially less than wedding gowns.

Previously Owned:

Many times you can find a true bargain on a designer gown that was worn once by someone else. This practice is becoming much more common with the high prices of designer gowns. Many brides will wear the gown for the ceremony and receiving line, then change into something more comfortable for the reception and dancing.

They will then offer to sell their gowns to one of the many places that recycle bridal apparel and recoup some of their original cost. You might be able to find something really special at a heavily discounted price.

Check out these sites:
- www.PreOwnedWeddingDresses.com
- www.OnceWed.com
- www.RecycledBride.com
- www.WoreItOnce.com

Borrow Something Old:

If you are so inclined, ask your mother or other relative if you could use their wedding dress. In many cases they had these dresses cleaned, sealed and stored since their own weddings. Ask to see their wedding photos and if you liked their dress, it might be a viable, low cost alternative to purchasing a new wedding gown.

You will also fulfill the "something old" and "something borrowed" parts of the time honored tradition "something old, something new, something borrowed and something blue" which was once thought to give the bride good luck, fertility and prosperity. It still remains something that many families honor within their wedding traditions.

Avoid Alteration Expansion:

Alteration prices can increase your net cost by as much as 25 to 35 percent in some cases. To minimize the alteration expansion costs, look for gowns that look great just the way they are. Don't try to transform an existing dress into something that it is not. The added alterations could put you over your budget quickly.

Dis-Embellish:

The higher the degree of embellishment, lace, taffeta and beading that your dress has, the higher the cost. If you really love a dress that is highly embellished, ask if they have the same dress with little or no embellishment.

In some cases, you will find that they have the same design, but it is made with a less expensive fabric. This may be just the answer to your design needs and then you can use your accessories to dress up the gown to meet your personal desires.

No Junk in this Trunk:

A trunk show is where many designers offer their collections through certain bridal boutiques with a variety of purchase incentives. These incentives could be cost savings or free accessories, etc. But do your homework and research the dresses you are interested in before the show. Most of the incentives that are offered only apply during that specific visit and show.

De-Tuxify The Groomsmen:

Groomsmen can also help with the savings. A sharp men's dress suit can cost nearly as much as the rental of a designer tuxedo and shoes. Talk with your groomsmen and suggest that they each buy a matching suit of your selection, along with a shirt and color coordinated ties.

Their entire outfit may cost slightly more, but they own and reuse a good suit many times over. If you find some of the better department store designer suits on sale, you can usually negotiate an even lower price for the purchase of 4-8 suits. You may need to reach out past the salesperson to a store manager, but I have witnessed some really great bargains with this method.

My own son, with his mother's help found a $500 suit for less than $160 after all discounts were applied. I also took one in a different color and they were happy to honor the same price as the wedding party.

For great variety of colors and low prices on men's ties, take a look at this online source. I have ordered many ties over the years and their service, quality, selection and prices are great. They also deliver very quickly in the United States.

The Tie Guys - http://www.tieguys.com

Action Summary:

Little things can add up to big expenses, especially with the formal wear for weddings. If you are serious about saving money on your wedding, the wedding gowns, bridesmaid dresses and grooms-men's attire can be an area for concern and a great opportunity.

By using the resources in this chapter, you can easily shave your budget and provide added value to your entire wedding party. By keeping an open mind and asking the right questions, you can easily cut costs and look great.

Your $500.00 Challenge:

How can I (we) use this information to save at least $500.00 on our wedding attire?

Chapter 3: Invitation & Thank You Savers

Another area that can balloon your wedding expenses is all the printed materials that go into the wedding process. With save-the-date cards, wedding invitations, menu cards, ceremony programs, place cards, and then thank-you cards, the average printing costs for a 150 person wedding are estimated between $750 to $3,000. That is before postage which can add another $200.

But the good news is that you can do it for substantially less and achieve some great results. With a little time and research, you can save hundreds and even thousands of dollars by using one or more of the suggestions below. Please be sure to review all items in this chapter before ordering anywhere. Some of these cost savers are tips-within-a-tip and can compound your savings.

Make your own:

Many young couples have a very unique vision of what their wedding and wedding invitations should look like. If you have a good drawing program and a specific idea that you are trying to convey, it may be easy for you to design, edit and print your own invitations. The paper and printing choices are readily available from most office supply stores and you know your creations will be unique and one-of-a-kind.

Use fiverr.com: https://www.fiverr.com

I have used fiverr.com for many things over the years. There are some really talented designers around the world and you can access them from this service. Base projects are only $5.00 (plus a $1.00 processing fee for fiverr.com) and there are currently hundreds of designers that offer wedding invitation packages.

Many of them offer an upgrade for an additional $10.00 to $50.00 that will include table cards, thank-you cards etc. Look at their previous designs and see if they have something you like or can modify. Setting up a Fiverr.com account is free and even if you don't like the first designer's work, for $5.00 you can try another.

Try Etsy.com: https://www.etsy.com

Etsy is an open marketplace for all kinds of wedding ideas, products and services. Invitations and design sets are no exception. There are over a hundred thousand designs on Etsy and you can sort them by price, most recent and relevancy. You will find some great deals and plenty of ideas to make your invitations special.

PDF It:

Find a graphic designer to design your invitations and ask them to provide a high resolution PDF of your designs. Then take your designs to a local print shop or one of the online printing services listed below. All that you have to do next is assemble the invitations and get them ready for delivery.

Online Printing Services:

Online printing services can be a great way to get your invitations for less. Most have their own templates for you to modify, then print. You can always upload your own design from others sources and just pay for the printing. Here are a few of the top picks, they all offer great prices, selections, quality and fast turnaround:

Next Day Flyers	http://www.nextdayflyers.com
4OVER4.com	http://www.4over4.com
U-Printing	http://www.uprinting.com
Overnight Prints	https://www.overnightprints.com
48 Hour Print	https://www.48hourprint.com
Vista Print	http://www.vistaprint.com

Ask for Help:

A great way to save on your invitations is to ask for help from a guest that you know has graphic design skills. Ask them to design your invitations and other printed needs in lieu of giving you a wedding gift. Their skill and connections in the business may help you save the entire cost as they may get professional discounts from their suppliers.

If they are not in the design business, but are very comfortable and talented, you can offer to have them do your design and then provide the camera ready artwork or high resolution PDF. You can then send to one of the online printing services above or to your local print shop.

All at Once:

Another way to save is to order all your printing needs at once. If you order them one at a time and pay shipping on each item, you will not receive quantity discounts or preferred shipping rates. If the order size is large enough, many online services offer free shipping options if you are not in a rush.

Scrap the Save-The-Date:

If you are not worried about your family and friends being overbooked on your wedding date, skip the save-the-date cards or magnets entirely. You will save between $100 to $300 on printing and postage. Just send them an email, text, phone call or personal visit and ask them to reserve your wedding date. The word will travel fast in most families.

Postcard it:

You can also save by utilizing a postcard for guest responses instead of the response card and envelope. While the printing costs are not significantly cheaper between the 2 options, the postage is. A postcard can be mailed for $0.35 versus a first class envelope at $0.49 each.

Trash the Tissue:

Skip the tissue paper between layers. Years ago it was necessary to stop the ink from bleeding or smudging. Today, the inks are significantly better and this is no longer an issue. The cost is small, but if added to the other savings, it all adds up.

Skip the interior envelopes as well for the same reasons. Everything can and should be placed inside the one mailing envelope. There is no need for additional envelope costs or potentially the higher mailing costs that can be incurred if your invitation packet goes over the 1 ounce weight limit.

Think Outside the Square:

For some reason the post office has rules that make many square wedding invitations subject to a surcharge because their sorting machines and scanners are not set up to process them. There is a $0.21 surcharge for using any size or shape that is non-machinable.

This can add up quickly on top of the postage and printing costs. Avoid square envelopes or be prepared to pay extra.

Digital Delivery:

You can now have your invitations delivered digitally to each of your invited guests. I believe this method will become more popular every year. You can customize a wide array of templates and then send via email. You save printing, postage and they even offer some great information reporting.

Their tools include: RSVP and plus-one tracking, open-rate management, registry announcement, wedding website links, photo sharing, and even survey questions to collect meal preferences, allergies or song requests.

Your guests will appreciate the electronic save-the-date which can easily reference details and information via their phone or email. The electronic version will also allow them to immediately add your big day... to their calendars!

Prices are based on how many invitations you will be sending and are quite reasonable. Here are two of the main companies offering this digital delivery service:

GreenVelope   https://www.greenvelope.com

PaperlessPOST   https://www.paperlesspost.com

Action Summary:

With all the money that you can spend for a wedding, it is a great idea to make cuts where you can. We have shown you how to reduce invitation costs in a variety of ways. Now it is up to you to select the methods that best fit your style and budget.

Your $200 to $500.00 Challenge:

How can I (we) use this information to save at least $200 to $500.00 on our wedding invitations, programs and other printing needs?

Chapter 4: Venue & Date Savers

Finding ways to save on your venue can entail being open-minded, creative and flexible with the details, ambiance and timing. Her are a nice array of alternative suggestions that will save money and still offer a great experience.

Skip Saturday:

Because Saturday is the most common day to get married, it also will be the most in demand and the most expensive. If you can find a Friday or Sunday that works for you, you might be able to save up to 50% because these are days the venue would not have normally booked.

You do have to ask for a discount and make sure that they can be properly staffed, but the savings can be very significant. While we are talking about dates, any other days of the week can be a possibility. Just remember that family and friends will generally be working and may not stay late or drink as much during the week. This can also save money if properly planned.

Don't overlook Monday through Thursday either. Your friends and loved ones will come on any day if they know you are getting married and trying to avoid the high costs.

Go Small Town:

It is just common sense that if you get married in a big city like New York, Chicago, Boston or San Francisco, you will most likely pay a lot more than if you get married in Poughkeepsie, Rockford, Lowell or Walnut Creek.

Having Your wedding in a small town versus the "Big City" can save you a bundle. Because the venues in smaller towns serve smaller populations, they may have more openings and much lower overhead and costs. It is not uncommon to save as much as

$10,000 by switching from a Big City to the Small Town.

Wake-Up Weddings:

One of my favorite ways to save is to have a Morning wedding. Most venues will be happy to accommodate your morning wedding and have you on your way by Noon or 2:00PM. You can have some great breakfast food buffets that your guests will love and the costs can be less than half the cost of a dinner or luncheon.

You will also save money on liquor costs as most guests will drink less alcohol. If you find a venue/restaurant that holds a fancy Sunday, Mothers Day or Easter brunch buffet, ask if they can accommodate a group of 100, 200, etc. Don't mention that it is a wedding until you get their prices for a large "party" breakfast buffet.

Another benefit is that the wedding party and guests will be rushed to get ready early in the morning, show up fresh and sober. Chances are that you will have a great start and a wonderful set of memories as well.

Afternoon Reception:

If you would like to reduce costs, try holding a 2:00PM afternoon reception with hors d'oeuvres, champagne and cake. If you can eliminate a full meal in lieu of small appetizers and drinks followed by cake and coffee you will reduce your reception catering costs by over 50% or more. This can be a great alternative with a very chic and modern theme.

Off Season:

Spring and Summer weddings are the hot spot for venues. Most couples prefer to get married during the warm weather and blossoming flora. By choosing to schedule your big day in the off-season, you can negotiate a much lower price for the same wedding packages.

Negotiation Tip: Start by asking for their prime season pricing and calendar of dates available. Then ask if there is any way they can reduce their price by 50%. They may suggest their off season dates and a price reduction of 25% to 40% as a counter offer.

This will give you a baseline for when to schedule your wedding and a price list that can significantly reduce your costs.

Local Church:

If you or your significant other are a member of a local church parish, consider asking to rent their congregation meeting room for your wedding reception. By holding the ceremony at the church and then proceeding directly to the parish meeting room, you can save thousands of dollars.

Many of these church meeting rooms have modern kitchens that a caterer can use and in some cases, you can even ask if the church has a women's auxiliary group that caters home-style cooking for the meal.

With this arrangement, you can accommodate a reasonably large party with good food, some alcohol, music and dancing at a very reasonable cost.

Small Reception:

Another great way to save money is to hold a very small intimate wedding ceremony with a small reception following. Then a few days, weeks or months later, hold a big party for everyone that you would like to have invited.

The big party can be casual and allow you to mingle with all your guests in a more relaxed atmosphere. The costs for a outdoor party or to rent a fire hall can be much less expensive than the formal wedding venues that you will encounter.

The big party can have a wedding theme and many of your guests will bring wedding gifts even if you ask them not to. Family and friends can contribute by making favorite dishes and desserts and you can offer to provide the entrees, beer and wine.

Who doesn't love a big party with family and friends?

Only One Location:

Having your ceremony and your reception at the same location can save time, transportation and money as well. While a Catholic Priest or Rabbi may not be able to perform the ceremony outside their place of worship, many other officiants can and will.

If you can find a location that can accommodate a ceremony and a reception, you will easily save the costs associated with using separate venues for each.

As an added bonus, your guests will only need to travel to one location which will save time and allow for the party to begin immediately following the ceremony.

Guests will not have to find activities to occupy themselves between the events. If you are having a 2:00 PM ceremony with a 5:00 PM reception, that can be a long day with a lot of mildly inconvenienced and disgruntled guests.

Court House Wedding:

Having your wedding at a court house doesn't have to be like a visit to your local county clerk's office. Try to find a beautiful, historic court house in your area and make the arrangements to hold your ceremony (and possibly even your reception) there.

You may have to limit the number of guests, but you can still have everyone beautifully dressed for photos. Court houses are budget friendly and they are very efficient with all the paperwork and guidance.

You can then focus more attention on your reception and expand your guest list to accommodate your desires.

To find local courthouses, Google search – town court house - and you will see the local ones for your area.

Rent A House:

Consider renting a large vacation home to accommodate your wedding and reception party. The cost to rent a beautiful house for a week or weekend could be substantially less than the cost of an average wedding venue.

You will probably want to keep it on the smaller size, rather low-key, bring in a caterer and some alcohol. If you have it for the week or weekend, you can offer your wedding party or family the opportunity to stay in the guest rooms instead of driving or a hotel.

It could be a nice vacation getaway along with the events of your big day.

Restaurant Reception:

Another cost saving and fun idea is to invite all your guests to a fancy restaurant for dinner and dancing after the ceremony. This can be a great reception for a lot less than it would cost to hold the entire reception at a wedding venue.

Obviously you will want to make arrangements with the restaurant so they can accommodate your party. Make sure they will have enough cooks, bartenders and service staff on duty to meet the increased demands.

You will be using there facilities, decor and menu but if planned properly, you will save a bundle. Just make sure that they will allow you to bring in a cake for your special day.

Non-Traditional Locations:

An open mind and an open heart can lead you on a path to anywhere. Parks, Beaches, Art Gallery, Bed and Breakfast's can all be great locations for a wedding ceremony and a reception.

While these non-traditional locations may take some additional decorations and planning, the cost savings can be quite dramatic.

Many public parks and beaches are free to visit and may charge a small fee to rent a shelter in advance to secure your date and location.

The opportunities are limited only by your imagination. You never know if it can work... unless you ask. Make a few calls and don't always take the first "NO" as the final answer.

Back Yard Barbecue:

If you, a relative or a friend have a beautiful spacious back yard that you think would be a great location for a wedding... ask.

They may be honored and excited that you would consider using their back yard.

Make sure to keep them involved in all the details and ask for their input and suggestions. Especially when it comes to bathrooms, parking and use of their house or other facilities.

Make sure to offer to repair any damage that is done to their yard or property in advance as a gesture of respect and assure them that you are not anticipating any outrageous behavior.

Make sure your guests know the ground rules before the wedding and have a sober friend or family member oversee all activities and shut down any unacceptable acts.

Brand New Venues:

If there is a new venue opening up in your area, stop by or give them a call. Ask if they have any wedding reception special deals. If they are looking to build their business quickly, they may be offering their services at very low margins to their first customers.

Because lead times for weddings are usually about 9 - 15 months in advance, they may have a lot of open dates waiting to be filled. Don't forget to ask for a better deal. If they lose your booking, they may not get another one, especially if the date is closer than 9 months away.

New businesses know that building a reputation takes time, and word of mouth referrals are the best form of advertising. Offer to spread the word if you like the service, food and ambiance... for a discount.

If you don't ask... you will never know.

College Campus:

Most college campuses have some great dining halls. If you recently graduated from the school or know someone connected with the campus, ask if you can get married there. If the answer is yes, the price is usually a bargain.

With a little decorating and the right menu, you and your guests will be treated to a campus experience that will be remembered forever.

If you are fortunate enough to have a local university that offers a culinary or hospitality program, ask if they would be interested in hosting your wedding as part of their student training program.

This is just the kind of hands on experience that their instructors would love to offer. You can rest assured that the students and their mentors will be offering some great menu selections to show off their skills.

You never know who knows who... until you ask... and put it out there.

All Inclusive:

Some venues will negotiate with their own suppliers to provide an entire wedding package at a very reasonable price. They provide everything. Decorations, flowers, food, liquor, music, photographer, cake, etc.

The price is usually a bargain, but you give up some control over the individual items. If you are not concerned about every little detail being perfect to your specifications, these can be a great savings opportunity.

Action Summary:

As you can see, this chapter offers a wealth of saving ideas for your dates and venues. One key to finding these is to take your time, ask friends and relatives for ideas and then explore anything that looks interesting to you. Once you settle on a concept, day, date, time and location, the rest of your plans will fall into place nicely.

Your $500.00 to $1,000.00 Challenge:

How can I (we) use this information to save at least $500.00 to $1,000.00 on our reception venue?

Chapter 5: List and Party Savers

One of the best ways to save money is to cut the size of your guest list. Just cutting it down from 200 to 150 will save money in a variety of areas. You will save money on invitations, meals, liquor and even table centerpieces.

The main thing to focus on when putting your list together is add everybody at first... then begin cutting it down. Group your guests by categories, family, friends, co-workers, neighbors, parent's friends and parent's co-workers, etc.

Who will add value to the memories that will be made on your big day?

Those that make the final list should be individuals that when you ask the above question... their name is a resounding ...YES! Start by considering the following items.

Maximum Guest List:

Start by putting together your complete guest list. Include anyone that you feel would be invited if there was no limit on who you could invite. This will be the starting point for your process of elimination.

Once you know the largest possible number of guests that may be on your invitation list, you can begin looking at ways to modify and adjust it. Now the fun begins. Expect a few disagreements as you proceed through the next few steps. Just try to remember that it is a discussion and a process.

Your objective is to reduce the guest list down to a reasonable number and then begin planning your wedding around that desired target.

Brides Maids and Groomsmen:

Having a large wedding party can be a lot of fun, but it also adds cost to your wedding budget. The larger the party, the more it will cost for wedding party gifts, rehearsal party meals and drinks, invitations and meals for bridal party, their dates and parents if you choose to invite them along with several other costs, that incrementally increase as the size of your list gets larger.

Try to reduce your wedding party to the smallest number possible. If that means only the best man and maid of honor, that will work. If there are brothers or sisters of the bride and groom that need to be added, keep it to a minimum. A special friend or two that you feel are very important, add them. But keep it down to a minimum.

Most of these people will be invited as guests even if they are not part of your wedding party, so they will be there to share in your big day. The difference is that it will cost you $100 to $500 extra for each individual that you include in the wedding party. An extra 10 people could cost you between $1,000 and $5,000.

Unresponsive Relatives:

Keeping your list lean is a challenge. Some families believe that they have to invite every family member and relative in order to be politically correct.

The good news is that times have changed. If there are family members that you don't see or don't believe would add value to your wedding... remove them from the list. Chances are that they will not be upset, may not even care or might be relieved they were not invited.

Remember that the ideal guests at your wedding should be happy to be there and honored to be part of your wedding memories. They should be willing to participate, dance and have fun with your family, friends and others.

If you know someone will not share in this spirit, you are probably smart to leave them off the list. You will save money, headaches and hard feelings.

Friends:

Every one of our friends has to be invited to the wedding. Along with their significant other.

While this may be ideal, it is probably unrealistic unless you have only a few close friends.

All your high school, college, social, music and/or athletic group friends could take up your entire list. But would they all be classified as ideal guests. Probably not.

You will need to eliminate many people in an effort to reduce the overall size of your wedding. This can be more of a challenge than with family. Friends that make the big list usually are someone that you have fun with, otherwise they would not have made the first cut. The following categories will address how to eliminate and finalize your invitation list.

Neighbors:

We grew up together and spent many hours, days and years at each others houses, kitchen tables and backyards. The most important questions to ask are:

Would they be offended if they were not invited?

Would they have fun, participate and enjoy being there?

Are they a big enough part of my past, current... and future life?

Depending on your answers to these questions, the decision should be easy... or easier.

School Friends:

His college buddies, her college teammates and roommates, our BFF from high school... do they make the cut?

It depends on the same questions above:

Would they be offended if they were not invited?

Would they have fun, participate and enjoy being there?

Are they a big enough part of my past, current... and future life?

These answers will help eliminate names and continue to condense your list.

Social, Music or Athletic Group Friends:

My choir group, our co-ed soccer team, her toastmasters group, his fantasy football group, her pilates/yoga class and any other social group friends can be decided upon by using the same 3 questions above. A couple additional questions will help make this easier:

Would they expect to be invited?

Would they feel obligated to come if invited?

The answers to these questions will help decide who, and if, they should make the final list.

Co-workers:

If you have been working with the same people for quite a while now, you may have a few really great co-workers and a few that you just don't care for.

If you invite one, you have to invite them all... or do you?

You can use the same 3 questions above to help narrow down the field, but you need to look at a few more questions as well.

If they are not invited... will it negatively impact my current job?

Will it negatively impact my career or future advancements?

Will it create a hostile work environment moving forward?

The answers to these questions will help you decide who should, and should not be invited.

Parent's Friends:

Our parent's have their own list of friends that they want invited. How do we decide on these people?

The biggest question that you need to ask is...

Are our parents paying for all or some of the wedding costs?

If the answer is YES, then we need to make sure to get our parent's input on the names that they have added before we delete any. They should be asked the same questions as above.

If the answer is NO and we are paying for the entire wedding ourselves, then you can make the decision on your own. Make sure to let your parents know what you decided and that you had to limit the size because of cost factors.

Parent's Co-workers:

Our parent's also have some of their co-workers on the list. This can be a little more complicated as to who will make the final list. As above, the answer to whether your parents are paying for all or some of the wedding should be considered. But even if they are not paying for any of the wedding costs, you should ask them to answer these questions before you make your final decision.

If they are not invited... will it negatively impact your parent's current job?

Will it negatively impact your parent's career or future advancements?

Will it create a hostile work environment for your parent's moving forward?

While these are probably less connected than your own co-worker questions, if there are some people that you believe should be invited to help your parent's future work situations, it would be advisable to do so.

Action Summary:

The key to keeping your list under control is to be flexible and open minded. Ask enough pertinent questions about any questionable guest before removing them from the final list.

A good list is one that when you look at the names... you smile and get excited to see them at your big day. There may be a few people that are "required" to be invited, but don't let these decisions impact your fun and happiness.

Your $500.00 to $1,000 Challenge:

How can I (we) use this information to save at least $500.00 to $1,000.00 by controlling the size of our wedding invitation list?

Chapter 6: Dance Music Savers

Finding great music for dancing at your wedding is not difficult. But doing it in a way that keeps the cost down can be a challenge. I will share some of the best ideas that I have seen or heard about that will make the process easier.

Venue's Sound System:

Check to see if the venue that you are using has a built-in sound system or a portable one that you can use. In many places they do, as it is something that they provide for business meetings and seminars.

If they have them available, ask if you can use it for your wedding reception at no additional cost. If they agree, make sure to arrange a convenient time for you and your designated DJ to visit and learn how to use their system.

Then all you need to do is select your playlist and let the dancing begin.

Be Your Own DJ:

If you would prefer to mix the music yourself, you can easily ask your invitees for music that will get them up on the floor when they send back their RSVP. You can also ask them for songs that would keep them in their chairs as well.

Once you review the list and preferences, you can download the songs into a playlist and you could just let it play all night long from your tablet or laptop. But this can be a bit of a distraction for you to manage. So I suggest one of the following methods to free you up for all the fun.

Ask A Friend... For A Friend:

Everyone has a friend that would be a great DJ because they are funny and have a great personality. But if they are really a friend, they will probably be on your guest invitation list. So it wouldn't be right to ask them to spend your entire wedding as your DJ for the electronic tunes.... BUT....

You could ask that friend (or others) if they had a friend, preferably someone that is not in your circle of friends that they would recommend as a DJ for your reception. In many instances you can offer them dinner and drinks and that will suffice. In some cases it may cost you $50 to $100 for the evening.

Either way it can be a big cost saver over the $1,000 average cost of a commercial DJ and sound system. It is an even greater savings over the $3,500 you would pay for a live band.

Find an MC – Master of Ceremony:

If you know the tunes you want played and have already put together your playlist on a digital device, all you need is someone to start and stop the music during the reception events. The rest of the night they can just let it play and add some comments as they see the action unfolding.

But where can you find someone to do this if you have exhausted all your connections and friends of friends? Where can you find someone that is comfortable in front of a group and talking with a microphone? Where can you find someone that is entertaining and humorous who would be willing to help you out?

Reach out to your local Toastmasters groups and ask if they have anyone that would like to be a Wedding DJ for the evening. You will provide the sound system, playlist, dinner and a small stipend if they get up and run the show.

Toastmasters International is a worldwide non-profit organization that teaches public speaking and leadership skills.

Being a Toastmaster myself, I can guarantee that there are probably 3 to 5 members in each club that would be great and would love the opportunity to practice their DJ and Masters of

Ceremony skills at your wedding reception.

Many would probably do it for the free meal and a few drinks, but if you offer to pay a small stipend, my guess is you will have your choice of a few good men and women.

To find a list of clubs in your area, you can visit the Toastmasters.org website and click on the "Find a Club" link at the top of the page. Enter your address in the location box and you will see how many local clubs are in your area.

When I enter my address, there are 24 local clubs within a 25 mile radius. Here is the direct link to the Toastmasters International website: http://www.toastmasters.org/Find-a-Club

Use Spotify Premium:

If you want to download high quality songs and put together a great playlist without trying to find all the songs online or from CD's, try using Spotify Premium, Apple Music or Deezer Premium.

Each of these services offers a 30 day Free trial and once you are set up, you can choose from a library of over 30 million songs. You can download them to a hard drive and play them offline which is a great idea. You wouldn't want to have the internet or your wireless signal go down during the festivities.

After the 30 day Free trial period it is just $9.99 per month and you can cancel at any time. Check them out at the sites below or via Google search.

Spotify Premium: https://www.spotify.com/us/premium/

Apple Music: http://www.apple.com/music/

Deezer Premium: https://www.deezer.com/offers/

Bluetooth Wireless Tailgate Speaker:

If your venue doesn't have a sound system that you can tap into and you cannot find a friend that has a wireless or wired speaker system you can borrow for the reception, there are a bunch of relatively inexpensive speaker systems that will provide plenty of sound for even a large reception hall. Here are a few that I have seen and used for a multitude of party functions. These are each around $100 and will provide plenty of quality sound.

ION Audio Tailgater (iPA77)   http://a.co/g9cuUK1

iLive ISB665B Bluetooth Tailgate Speaker   http://a.co/4308vLW

ION Audio Tailgater Express   http://a.co/3Kf5llw

I am sure you can find plenty more by searching Amazon or Google. Before you buy one, ask a friend that does a lot of tailgating or outdoor parties. They may already have one charged up and ready to go.

Music & Playlist Suggestions:

If you are putting together your own playlists, here are a few things to consider as you are selecting, organizing and saving your files.

1. Make a playlist of your First Dance song, the Father/Daughter song and the Mother/Son song that will be played to start the evening off.

2. Make a another short playlist of your first 5 songs that you want to play. These will be the ones that get the party started and get your guests up on the floor.

3. Make a general, longer playlist that includes a nice mix of fast dancing, then a couple slow dance songs in a row and then keep mixing it up for guests of every age.

4. Finally make sure to have a playlist with your final 3 songs. These will be played when you get to the end of the night and everyone is winding down. You want to give them the final 3 that will get everyone back on the floor to finish the night with a bang.

Make sure to let your DJ/Master of Ceremony know which ones to play and when. If you plan it properly you will run out of time before you run out of music.

Be sure to consider the fast and slow dancing songs based on the age and demographics of your wedding guests. You wouldn't want to leave out your parents and grandparents if you are lucky enough to have them present.

Action Summary:

These are just a few of the ways that you can cut the cost of your dance music. Of course you can find an online special for a commercial DJ or try to win one at the Bridal shows. If you really want to leave your own mark on the music, dance floor and make sure that your songs are played... do it yourself and celebrate your style.

Your $500.00 Challenge:

How can I (we) use this information to save at least $500.00 on our Dance Music and DJ?

Chapter 7: Photography & Video Savers

Photographs and video are a great keepsake and memories for every wedding couple. With the average cost for a photographer around $2,500 and another $900 for a videographer, that is another fairly large cost that many young couples cannot easily afford.

In this chapter I will share some ways to reduce that cost and possibly have more interesting and possibly better, photos and video to add to your wedding memories.

Limit Coverage:

If you can find a photographer that will offer a limited coverage package, you can save quite a bit of money. Limited coverage usually means that you have them show up for the pre-wedding photos, the ceremony and a brief session right after the ceremony. This will take 3 to 4 hours compared to the entire day which usually takes 6 to 8 hours.

The problem is that during the peak wedding season, most photographers will not take a limited coverage contract, because if they do, they might lose out on a full day, full coverage wedding which is much more profitable.

If you are planning to hold your wedding in the non-peak season or on any other day than a Friday or Saturday during the peak season... Ask for a limited coverage package deal. You will normally save $500 to $1,500 off their full package.

Digital vs. Prints:

If you pay your photographer to provide the digital rights to your wedding photos, you can select the ones you want and print them yourself. Skip the costly print packages and albums that they provide and make your own. You can find great wedding albums on Amazon, Shutterfly and many other online sources.

You can pick and choose from all your photos, then prepare your own wedding album, parent's albums and even provide wedding party albums for less than you will pay to have a professional photographer compile them for you.

Make sure to get the printed and signed digital rights release form from your photographer. You will need to make copies of this form for anyone that is printing your photos.

Take 1... Not 2:

Many wedding photographers like to have 2 photographers covering your wedding to help avoid mistakes and shoot photos from multiple angles. If their standard package includes this assistant photographer, you can ask if there is a discount for only one photographer.

If they charge extra for the additional photographer, you can reduce the cost by choosing a single shooter. In many cases, the assistant is a photographer in training and is there more to help carry the equipment than for their photographic excellence.

Book a Pre or Post Wedding Shoot:

Another great option to reduce cost and stress is to book a Pre-Wedding or Post-Wedding photo shoot. This is where you have the bride and groom schedule a photo session on a weekday, usually Monday through Thursday, before or after the wedding.

If you can get the entire bridal party and/or both families available for this scheduled session, this can make for a some great, low stress photos with studio quality, great outdoor or spectacular indoor backgrounds.

Everyone dresses elegantly as if they were at the actual wedding and there are no time constraints on getting great shots. Photographers like these sessions because they are additional jobs and the participants are usually sober and focused on getting good photos.

You must ask the photographer if they offer these packages and make sure to get a discount that is acceptable. Photographers generally will not advertise these off peak discount packages, but once you ask, they will be very reasonable on what they offer.

Book a Newbie:

If you can find a new photographer that is just breaking into the business, you may be able to negotiate a good deal before they establish their reputation. Ask friends, co-workers and relatives if they know any new photographers that are good.

Many college art majors are into photography and upon graduation are looking to explore their creative side. Weddings have a very structured side, but also allow for individual creativity and expression. (See Fun Photo Ideas below)

You may even be able to negotiate an "at cost" contract with your newbies to help them build their wedding portfolio. If you ask and they say NO, you can continue to work your way upward with additional incentives. Start with free advertising at your wedding reception. Allow them to place their cards and a small display near your cake. Then add dinner and drinks. If needed, try a small stipend for travel expenses and keep working higher until they say YES.

Every photographer has to start somewhere with their first wedding. You can help them out and find yourself a great deal.

Your Own Hashtag:

If you want to see your wedding through the eyes of your family and guests, you have to make it easy for them to share their photos and videos with you. The easiest way to do this is to provide your own wedding Hashtag. These can be fun to create, but make sure you set it up before the wedding so you can begin sharing it with your friends and guests early.

You should also have your hashtag printed on your invitations, wedding program, table cards, photo booth and thank you cards after the wedding. Print it anywhere and everywhere that your guests may look to find it.

Your hashtag will make it easy to find the files as they are uploaded to Facebook, Instagram, Twitter and any other social media that your guests share. *(See Fun Photo Ideas below)*

<u>Note of Caution:</u> If your guests are sharing photos and video live from the wedding, it could be an invitation for online predators to figure out where you live and attempt to burglarize your home or apartment. It is always a great idea to have someone stay at your place during the wedding. Pay or ask one of your friend's brothers, sisters or parents to watch your house during the wedding and reception. Better safe than sorry.

Friends and Guests:

Ask your friends, family and guests to take photos throughout your ceremony and reception, then ask them to upload their images to your custom wedding hashtag on Facebook, Twitter, Instagram and other social media. It will be like having dozens of amateur photographers working for you taking candid shots everywhere.

They will definitely get shots that a professional photographer would have missed. The quality of their images may not be professional, but cell phone cameras have been getting better every year with great clarity and higher resolution.

You may need to crop the photos and edit a few items, but you will likely capture some great memories. And these photos are totally free for you to use. Your budget will love it.

Check the Newspaper:

No not for ads. Check the photographer names on the photo credits of your local newspapers and online news. These are professional photographers that may be interested in doing your wedding at a substantial discount. Call the paper and ask for them by name.

Compliment their news coverage photos and then ask if they ever do weddings on the side.

Many wedding photographers started as news photographers. They are trained and prepared to show up early, wait for the best shots, work the event, and wrap it up when they are done. They generally have access to great equipment and have plenty of experience covering big events.

Wedding Photo Apps:

While I think there are better ways to save money, I feel that I need to mention wedding photo apps as another method of savings.

There are dozens of wedding photo apps that will allow your guests to upload their photos and aggregate them for your viewing. Most are free to use, but most require you to pay a fee to have them downloaded or printed for offline viewing.

WedPics, AppyCouple, Yapp and several others are popular apps that can be explored. I believe that if you create your own great hashtag and make it known to your guests before and after the wedding, you will have a wonderful variety of great memories to share as you desire.

DIY Photo/Video Booth:

Making your own photo/video booth is a great idea and can save hundreds of dollars. You also get to add your creative touch and let your guests share their fun and wacky side.

Here are the 4 steps to a great photo/video booth:

1. *Backdrop:* Make a backdrop that you will want to see in the back of each photo and video. Some of the best include a sign or some other markings that indicate your wedding date, your names, your hashtag and maybe 1 photo of the wedding couple. If you search Google for - wedding photo booth backdrops - you will have plenty of great ideas. Try to set up this backdrop and lighting, in a noticeable, but

separated area of the reception venue. This will encourage guests, but not be in the way.

2. _Lighting:_ This is probably the **most important element** of the photo booth. If you don't have enough light and are relying on camera phone flashes, you will be disappointed by the results. Make sure that your photo booth is very brightly lit up. You can use a couple of those multi-bulb dorm room lights if they are around. Make sure to use compact fluorescent daylight bulbs or the newer LED bulbs if you have them.

Here are a couple inexpensive studio lighting kits that will be great for less than $100.

   - Julius Studio Lighting Kit: http://a.co/6BXVhlm

   - Lighting Kit by LimoStudio: http://a.co/3LaJChO

3. _Props:_ Get some props for your guests to use in their photos and videos. The wackier the better. Most people will use some of them and others will just take a nice photo or video with a message. My favorite prop is a Mini Chalkboard and chalk. A small Dry-Erase board with colored pens might be even better. This allows your guests to write you a brief note and have it included in their photo forever.

4. _Hashtag:_ Get your own wedding hashtag for all your friends to upload their photos and videos. If you don't include your hashtag, you will never be able to easily sort and collect all the photos and videos.

NOTE: It is a great idea to include your hashtag in your background somewhere so that your guests can upload and add the hashtag after the wedding or at home when they may be thinking clearer. This way they will have it handy in the photo or video that they took with their phone. Also place it in your wedding program or on their wedding place-cards.

Fun Photo Ideas:

From BuzzFeed: 42 Impossibly Fun Wedding Photo Ideas You'll Want To Steal – Here is the link: https://www.buzzfeed.com/peggy/impossibly-fun-wedding-photo-ideas-youll-want-to-steal?utm_term=.fe2rGB7XnE

From PopSugar: How to Create a Wedding Hashtag No One Else Will Have – Here is the link: http://www.geeksugar.com/Wedding-Hashtag-Ideas-34836983/

Action Summary:

In this chapter we have shared a variety of great ways to get those photographic and video memories recorded, uploaded and shared with you, your family, friends and guests.

You have to weigh the pros, cons and costs associated with having a professional photographer, an amateur photographer or your friends and guests capture these memories.

For many young couples, pictures and video are extremely important and everything has to be perfect. For others, they are just images of the big day and whatever we get will be great. You have to decide for yourself how much you are willing to spend to get those memories recorded. Whichever you decide, there are ways to save!

Your $500.00 Challenge:

How can I (we) use this information to save at least $500.00 on our wedding photography and video services?

Chapter 8: Time and Fun Savers

It is your big day....

Every minute counts....

The time you spend with your family and friends will be remembered for a lifetime.

Wouldn't it be nice if you had an extra 30, or even 60 minutes to share with all those that are so important to you?

As your wedding day approaches, you can make a handful of great decisions that will allow you to spend more time with your guests. Because... having fun and enjoying your big day is what it is all about.

Below are a few that you should discuss with your bridal party, family and wedding planning group as early as possible before your big day. Your efforts here will make a big difference.

Fully Embrace the Rehearsal:

Make sure that everyone that will be involved in any part of the ceremony attends the wedding rehearsal and understands their role. This includes the bride, groom, bridal party, parents, flower girl, ring bearer, photographers, etc.

Encourage everyone to ask questions if they have a concern or need clarification. This will make the ceremony run smoother and more efficiently, getting you on to the photos, reception and honeymoon with time to share.

The rehearsal can be a great place to hand out your Wedding Events Timeline to all the key people and make sure they are prepared and ready to keep your big day moving on-time and under-budget.

Wedding Events Timeline:

It can help save valuable minutes on every aspect of your wedding day plans. A wedding day timeline of events is a great way to help everyone from the bride and groom to the bridal party, family and guests to make sure they know what, when, where and how to get there.

Take some time, a few weeks before your wedding, to prepare a wedding events timeline. Make a PDF of your creation, then print and email it to everyone that is involved in your big day. It is a great way to eliminate confusion, delays and wasted time.

Here is a site that has over 35 free templates that you can download and use.

https://www.template.net/business/timeline-templates/wedding-timeline-template/

By searching Google or Pinterest, you will find thousands of other ideas and templates if you cannot find one in this group that you like.

Limit Your Group Photos:

Group photos can be the most frustrating and time consuming pictures to take. There is always someone missing, not smiling or making a funny face. While these may end up being perfect memories of the day, you don't want to let them delay your other planned events.

Prepare a "Must Have", a "Wish We Have" and "Please Do NOT" photograph list. Make sure that your wedding photographer gets these lists in advance and agrees to follow your guidelines. If they have any suggestions for deletions or additional photos, ask them to run them by you a few days or a week in advance.

For the most part, try to limit group photos to Just the Families, The Wedding Party and any other very specific groups that you feel are a must have.

If the group is less formal, a few shots could be arranged informally at the reception. Some of these may include, college or high school friends, sports teammates, co-workers, etc.

Another great time saver is know when to say "NO". Feel free to tell your photographer No if they are trying to arrange a group photo that just isn't that important or isn't coming together quick enough.

Appoint Two Family Members:

Rarely does the photographer or their assistant know both family members very well.

Days or weeks before the pictures are taken, appoint one family member from each family that knows the grandparents, parents, siblings, aunts, uncles and anyone else that will be in the group photos.

Ask these two individuals to be in charge of getting the family ready for their wedding family photos. These will generally happen immediately following the wedding ceremony and the less time spent "rounding up the relatives", the more time you will have at your reception.

It is generally good to ask and appoint a healthy, responsible adult that can aid and assist elderly family members and strongly encourage younger members to "Get in Line".

This person should be polite and friendly, but also respected and authoritative. They can make your group photos a short and pleasant part of your wedding day.

Right now, think of who those two people will be. Write them down for future use.

1. Bride's family organizer: 2. Groom's family organizer:

Limit Your Receiving Line:

A receiving line can be a lot of fun...

It can also take a lot of time if each of your guests stops to talk to every person in the line.

Having just the Bride and Groom is the most efficient way to manage the receiving line. But many young couples have the parents, grandparents and even the bridal party as part of the receiving line.

The more people that are in this line, the more time it will take away from your other activities.

Keep it short and sweet and allow your guests to be greeted and then have them visit with parents, grandparents or the bridal party elsewhere.

Five Minute Toast Limit:

Toasts and speeches can be humorous, sentimental and very special moments in your wedding. Generally, the best man and maid of honor make a toast. At many weddings, the father of the bride, or other family member will make a short toast the the married couple as well.

One of the biggest delays can be allowing one of these speakers to talk without a time limit. They can ramble on with all kinds of stories that may or may not be relevant to the married couple. If they have been sampling the alcohol before their toast, they may be even more long-winded.

It is a great idea to ask each of the speakers to limit their toast to a maximum time of 5 or 7 minutes. If each can follow these guidelines, then the dinner will be served hot and the reception can move forward. Then the rest of the evenings events will not be pushed back taking time away from your cake, dancing and fun.

Buffet Versus Sit-Down:

Selecting a sit-down dinner can be more relaxing and a more expensive option for your wedding dinner. But if you are looking to save time, a sit-down dinner will take longer to serve each course to all your guests.

A buffet style dinner will move much faster and allow more time for you and your guests to mingle, dance and have fun. If you have a great menu and serving staff, you can have everyone served and still have time for those who might like seconds before many would have received their first meal with a sit-down dinner.

Vendor Gratuity Envelopes:

A few days prior to your wedding, it is a good idea to prepare your vendor gratuity envelopes. It gives you plenty of time to note your desired gratuity amounts and then make sure that the services provided deserve the amount you allocated.

By having your envelopes labeled and ready before the wedding, you can make sure that they are handy when your big day arrives. It may be a good idea to have someone else be responsible for these envelopes as you will be quite busy.

You can instruct a parent, sibling or other responsible adult on who should receive what envelope and amount. If by chance you are not happy with some aspect of the vendors service and would like to change the amount enclosed, be sure to let this person know before they share the gratuity.

Taking this task off your wedding day "to-do" list will save time and allow you to focus your attention on having more fun with your guests.

Organize Those Bustle Ties:

If bustling your wedding gown will involve a lot of ties, it will save time and frustration to have each of the ties coordinated in advance. You can number or color code each tie with ribbon or a marker for quick and effective attachment.

For those lucky individuals responsible for bustling your dress, this will be a great time saver and will guarantee it is done quickly and correct the first time. It will keep the excitement and fun rolling and not cause any unnecessary delays.

It is also a good idea to do a quick practice run the day before with your maid of honor, mother or whomever you have appointed to help with bustling your wedding dress.

Action Summary:

This chapter was all about helping you to save time and enjoy your day. These items should all be reviewed with your wedding party in advance in an effort to make your big day go smoothly. The less distractions you encounter, the more time you will have to share with those special guests. Use these time savers wisely and you will make the most of your big day.

Your 30 to 60 Minute Savings Challenge: *(Priceless...)*

How can we use this information to save at least 30 to 60 minutes on our wedding day? Then spend those precious moments having more fun with our wedding guests.

Chapter 9: Book Two Preview

I hope you enjoyed the wedding cost savers in this first book. In book two of this series, **Cut Wedding Costs – The Big Day and Beyond**, you will find more great cost savings ideas for each of the following areas.

As with this book, I have compiled a variety of ways for you to consider reducing the high costs associated with a wedding. The first book helped get you started on the areas that will arise in the early stages of your planning. Book 2 will help you to cut costs for the actual wedding day and some really great opportunities for your honeymoon savings.

In Chapter 8 you will get my Financial Marriage Savers. This is a very condensed version of the third book in this series where I layout a nice financial road map for every newly married couple to help strengthen and stabilize your wedding vows and marriage.

Financial problems are the number one cause of divorce around the world. Chapter 8, your preview of Book 3 will help you to identify and diagnose problems before they arise. It will then offer focused and strategic suggestions on how to overcome these obstacles and keep your marriage moving in a positive direction.

Enjoy your journey. It will be exciting and fun!

Book Two: **Cut Wedding Costs – The Big Day and Beyond**

Table of Contents:

Chapter 1: Ceremony Savers

Chapter 2: Meal Savers

Chapter 3: Flower & Decoration Savers

Chapter 4: Drink Savers

Chapter 5: Cake & Dessert Savers

Chapter 6: Limo & Transportation Savers

Chapter 7: Honeymoon Savers

Chapter 8: Financial Marriage Savers

Book 2: **Cut Wedding Costs – The Big Day and Beyond**, along with my other life enhancing books can be found by visiting my **Amazon Author Page**.

Here is the direct link.   http://amazon.com/author/keithmaderer

About the Author

Keith Maderer is an author, a dynamic and humorous speaker, an entrepreneur and a 30+ year veteran of the financial services industry. He completed the Certified Financial Planner (CFP) program in 1990 and has been a Fee-Only Registered Investment Adviser operating in Orchard Park, NY which is a suburb in the Buffalo/Niagara Falls region - since 1989. He works with individuals, business owners, pension plans and trusts to help them **clarify** their goals, **solve** their problems and make **simpler** and better financial decisions.

He has been married to his high school sweetheart (Lori) for over 30 years (I hear she is up for sainthood) and has 5 adult children and 1 grandchild. He has been active in many local non-profit organizations and has served as a coach, League Commissioner and President of the Orchard Park Little League baseball program. He was the co-founder, President and team coach of the Orchard Park Youth Basketball Association and was the founder and managing director of the Maderer Foundation.

He actively volunteers in the District 65 Toastmasters International organization where he has served as President of both the Clarence Toastmasters and Larkin Leaders Toastmaster groups. He has achieved their highest designation of excellence in public speaking and leadership – the DTM (Distinguished Toastmaster Award) after only 4 years in the program.

He was the recipient of the Toastmaster's District 65 – Division A – Club President of the Year award in 2014 and the District 65 - Area Governor of the Year award in 2015. He was the first runner up in the District 65 International Speech Contest in 2016 and loves sharing stories, anecdotes and messages that help motivate and inspire others to achieve their own success.

His hobbies include Reading, Biking, Hiking, Photography, Golf, Disc Golf and playing with his grandchildren.

For more information about Keith Maderer or to sign up for his **VIP email list**, please visit his website at KeithMaderer.com

When you sign up for the **VIP email list**, you will receive first notification of future book launches and special offers exclusively for insiders. These may include, but may not be limited to:

1. Limited time - free download offers for Keith's books
2. Limited time - free download offers for other publications that we have negotiated.
3. First look previews and sample chapters of Keith's upcoming books
4. First look at articles and blog posts that Keith publishes.

Other Books By Keith Maderer

Please check out my other print and ebooks on **Amazon.com**, my Audiobooks on **Audible.com** and online courses on **Udemy.com**. (coming soon)

Cut Wedding Costs – Before The Big Day - Book 1:

Over 80 Ways To Save Money, Time and Frustration... Before Your Big Day
https://www.amazon.com/dp/B06XCVPPCZ

Life Insurance... Who Needs It?

What Life Insurance Agents may not tell you... but YOU need to know... Before you buy
https://www.amazon.com/dp/B01N39YX8Q

Simplify Your Estate – The Simple Problem Solvers

Common Sense Problem Solving Strategies for Baby Boomers... and Their Parents
https://www.amazon.com/dp/B01LXKLOM2

How Much House... Can I Really Afford?

Practical Tips to Avoid becoming "House Poor"
https://www.amazon.com/dp/B01FQ8RL0W

Simplify Your Estate – Basic Documents

Common Sense Estate Planning Solutions
http://www.amazon.com/dp/B009F4LXE4

How To Get Your College Education... For Less

Help Design Your Own Financial Aid Package
http://www.amazon.com/dp/1453820531

Your Opinion Matters

You are the only one that can let me know if this book is helping you with your decisions and search for a new home. I truly appreciate that you decided to purchase, read and act upon this information.

I have one small request. If you would kindly write a short positive review for this book on Amazon.com, it will help me to make changes, answer additional questions and offer further valuable solutions on this an other topics.

Please let me know specifically about how you plan to use the strategies to Cut your Wedding Costs, as well as any other items you found useful.

If you click the link below it will take you to Amazon where you can sign in and share your thoughts about this book. Thank you for your effort on my behalf. I truly appreciate your time and effort.

Click Here to Review: **Cut Wedding Costs – Before The Big Day – Book 1**

Then sign in to your Amazon account, select the book to review, write and post your review.

Your Review could be the deciding factor to help someone else decide to purchase this book and Cut their own Wedding Costs. Please share your thoughts.

Thank You.

Please Share on Social Media

Please feel free to share this book with friends, family and coworkers on Facebook, Twitter, Pinterest, Google+ or LinkedIn. Only by your word of mouth can indie authors like myself build a following that can help shape future projects and help others succeed and avoid these mistakes.

Just Copy and Paste this Text and Link below – **Thank you**

I just read this book – Great ways to Cut Your Wedding Costs and avoid a Financial Wedding Hangover - http://amazon.com/author/keithmaderer

Facebook Share - Click Here

Twitter Share – Click Here

Pinterest Share – Click Here

Google+ Share – Click Here

LinkedIn Share – Click Here